Wild Thoughts

OF AN

Authentic Soul

T. LE SURE

Austin Ink Studio
Los Angeles, CA

Dedication

This book is dedicated to my incredible support system of family and friends. I am beyond blessed to have such a solid foundation. Thank you daddy, for teaching me how to think critically and outside of the box. Thank you mommy, for showing me how to be fearless, love unconditionally, and how to make things happen no matter what obstacle may stand in my way. Thank you to my sister, who continually inspires me to walk in my truth and stand in my power. Thank you to my goddess group tribe, who continues to support me on my journey to self-actualization. Thank you to my students, who inspired me to create something real and authentic. You have taught me the value of being transparent and how to step beyond fear for the greater good of all. Thank you to all the young girls and women who through all of life's challenges, push through to live, love, and grow.

Thank you.

A special thank you to the people who donated money to help me fulfill my dream of becoming a published author.

A Sincere Appreciation To:

Felicia Bams

Tovarich Bourne

Leola Compton

Donna Davidson

Diana Delgado

Robert Duling

Lorraine Duling-Norwood

Shamaine Ford

Jamie Franklin

Ekaterina Fuller

Wilson Greer

Marlies Harris

Shannon Hawkins

Jeffrey James

Kimberly James

Tonia James-Holden

Kenya Jones

Dorothy V. Kincaid

Norwood King

Carlotta Leftridge

Daynesha Lewis

Sherree Lewis-De' Vaughn

Justin & Kimberly Lewis

Dayo Majekodunmi

Tonya Milner

Courtney Nabors

Kemi Polk

Arrianne Rainey

Ann Reeves

Hanifa Schlinger

Victoria Tesfamariam

Mary Tynch

Christiana Williams

Tai Williams

Eric Wright

Clarence Young

Table of Contents

Introduction

I have always enjoyed reflective writing, but until now, it has always been private. Much of what I would like to share, are poems about my struggles with life's dilemmas. I struggle to see women's stories being told in authentic ways and I want to bring to light the various issues plaguing women who at different points in their lives become very lost and disillusioned by the world around us. Looking for love in the wrong places and often intrigued by the idea of instant gratification; not understanding the beauty of patience, understanding, and evolving into one's true self through time and life learned lessons. Then there is the whole issue of the insecurities that fester within us due to poor romantic relationships. My poems reflect my highs and lows, and internal struggles with the world that I created, and the men I've dated. Also, you will discover my journey towards self-love and my love and appreciation for others. This is my outlet, and it has allowed me to heal through self-reflection and by taking the time to learn how to love and accept me authentically. I believe at the core of human existence, we are all searching for a love that is unbound. A love that is without constraints; that allows us to be free and express freely. Thank you for taking the time to read. While reading my journey, I would like you to write and reflect on your own personal journey through life by using the "Authenticity Journal," in the back of the book. Please refer to this journal daily to write and re-write your own story.

Chapter 1
A Woman's Demise

She wanders in a meaningless existence of

self-infliction and condemnation because of the insecurities that consume her rational being.

Boy after man,

she allows tarnishing her self-worth.

This is a woman's demise.

She is ostracized because she's misunderstood.

She's called every name in the book.

Bitch, hoe, slut...

No one knows just how deep these words cut.

Feelings of admiration from others because she comes off so happy,

so powerful and robust,

with an "I can do all" attitude....

If they only understood that the true culprit of her destruction lies within her soul.

And her ability to withhold stories untold.

Afraid to express a sense of vulnerability, she hides behind a fake facade of confidence and power.

Calculating her every word, step and verb.

Methodical in her approach to taking over the world.

She revels in her dysfunction because it adds so much spice to her life. The continuous cycle of loveless pleasures contributes to her life of strife... Aesthetically sublime, internally blind. If you know this woman, please help her before she falls...

she's one day away from running out of time.

Chapter 2
I Hide

I hide behind my hair

So curly and cute

Makes the boys stare and tell me,

"Baby, I want to be with you."

I hide behind my makeup-conceal-her is my friend

I conceal so many bruises and insecurities behind my covered-up skin

I hide behind my clothes-picking out just the right fit

Just to fit in

One hundred likes on I.G...you go girl!...got the attention of the men!

I hide behind my degrees....1.....2... 3... you can't stop me!

I'm the Master's degree big shot! Hmmm.....not!

I hide behind my car, a Lexus IS

Oh, you didn't know?

No, I don't have money that flows, but let me put on this show

Because I know that when you see me

Step out this black on black with the tint,

You're going to look at me, like damn she's the shit!

Baby is cute in the face, slim in the waist, has a bounce in her curls,

two advanced degrees; she doesn't need me

Look at her in her sexy car to match

Yeah, she's a good catch

That's what they say,

but why don't I feel this way?

Chapter 3
Bye Bye Pain

You don't care about me

So many times I was ready to leave

Pain so deep-It will take years to unbury

Relax, release the toxins that cumulated

from this relationship-so un-stimulated

lust, sex, passion, thrust

How did we have love with no trust?

I'm done feeling so hope-less

I'm done living without bliss

Everything you do is so selfish

All about you and your needs

That you never took time to feed me

Compassion, understanding, patience undemanding

Instead, I got the opposite of my worth

I felt less than a penny and

you left me so empty

Forget even being half full

Feeling like such a fool for you

But this pent-up frustration from a love untrue

Will soon be gone

Once I've gotten rid of you

Periodt!!!

Chapter 4
Lost In Love

Why do I lay here
Such a desolate soul?
Lost I am from the truth be told
Fear, anger, still I let him back in
Leave him, keep him, burn within
He is not the one for me
But I can't let him go you see
Even though the lows outweigh the highs
So hard for me to say goodbye
But once I finally do
To myself, I will be true

Chapter 5
Lost One

I've fought so hard for love

For a simple hug, kiss, affection, a feeling of appreciation

Only to feel dismissed

It's painful to let go this time

because I thought I had won the battle

but the truth is, I refuse to fight

Blow for blow

I am now ready to grow and let go of what does not flow

The difference this time is I know where I want to go

Like the Mya song, "I'll be moving ooooooonnn……."

Chapter 6
Chaos

Thoughts, ideas, and pain from loveless pleasures all swirling around in my head like a tornado ready to cause destruction. Understanding that I am under construction but can't help but feel this incredible urge to know what it is that I am supposed to do, without all the roadblocks, detours and speed bumps. Life is a beautifully unwritten scripted journey…so they say. We are the actors in the bigger scheme of a movie or play

full of adventure, romance, loss, life-learned lessons,

but I'm impatiently waiting in this painful process.

It's not all bad though.

I get to meet interesting people along the way,

see myself in different lights;

shine, shine on until dim lights ignite.

So, I will do my best to patiently wait for the moment of knowing my purpose by allowing life to keep flowing

Anticipating the right time for

birthing to life my ideas and insight.

Chapter 7
Feeling Lost/Toxic Relationships:

So many times, I have felt lost in life. I didn't know if I was coming or leaving. I was just here, reacting to whatever was thrown my way, but not really dealing with all my pain, my insecurities, or my confusion. I just continued to take on life blow by blow and continuously felt defeated. It took me having a man who was mentally ill come into my life and turned my world upside down. All my friends around me were settling down with their boyfriends and out of desperation, I met this guy online, rushed into a relationship, and moved him into my apartment. I had no idea that he was mentally ill. I started noticing odd behavior from him. He would pace back and forth while talking to himself. He would get major anxiety from being in the house and would have panic attacks. In public, he would accuse me of looking at other men and get angry with me. I didn't understand. He was hypersensitive and very paranoid. After a while, I started feeling uncomfortable and asked him to move out. He then started to threaten suicide and became very emotional. I continued to live with him out of fear of him hurting himself, and because I felt sorry for him. This is what I had always done. I allowed people to manipulate me to feel bad for them, and I put others before myself.

Fast forward three months later, and this man's behavior became more erratic and dangerous. He became verbally abusive and hostile towards me. I somehow found his mother's contact information, and when I contacted her, her response was, "I am not dealing with this again." I found out that this guy had a history of this type of relationship with women. I later checked his criminal background record and discovered that he had battery and assault on his record against his baby's mother. All I could think to myself was how did I get here? I realized that this guy was simply a heightened reflection of the buried issues and insecurities that I had within myself. No I wasn't a violent person, a manipulator, or a suicidal person, but I had attracted this person into my life because subconsciously this is what I felt I deserved. Someone that needed me to take care of them and help them and who did not treat me right or who could not bring anything to the table; someone who was mentally ill.

Once I was able to get out of this situation, I started to invest more into myself. I went to therapy and I got a life coach. I learned a lot about how I was coping with my unresolved issues and why I continuously found myself in these traumatic love situations. I began doing yoga, getting into meditation, writing out my negative stories, and turning them into positive ones. I do a lot of self-work because it's so easy to get lost in this world of dysfunction. If you find yourself in a constant cycle of negativity and dysfunction, it's time to go deep within to get to the root of the problem. Your life is a direct reflection of your inner thoughts and feelings. Pay close attention to who or what is popping up. Seek guidance and support. You must be willing to take steps to find "you" and heal "you." No one else will do it for you.

Chapter 8
Man of Wonder

Man of prestige

genius of mind

quick-witted humor

leaving others bewildered

Special gift to this world,

understanding the more deep-seated need of humanity

following the split between the sane and insanity

knowing we all walk the fine line

years spent in the struggle to give justice for the unjustly accused and misused

never feeling like you are doing enough

because you know that there is so far to go

So, you are not willing to settle for no

because you know that it can be done

With faith, truth and understanding as step one

gentle soul, hard exterior

no one can put a finger

on the depths of your soul, and how it's not all controlled by your ego

intellectually captivating

mastering the art of articulating

presenting stories, ideas thoughts based on truth as stimulating

stimulates people to act think and do

They couldn't handle stepping one day in your shoe

For you are a renaissance man

so many feed from the palm of your hand

therefore, you don't allow a lot in, even as friends......

but you let me in

At times, I feel closer than kin

I'm mesmerized by your strength, vision, persistence and will

to will a better world for our little boys and girls

scaffold and build the community piece by peace

He is courageous and fearless, yet a gentle soul of mystique

Chapter 9
Power Woman

If I could just step into your shoes

If I could just step into your shoes

The power you possess is seamless,

Uncontested, you are invested in growth, knowledge, and wisdom

You radiate fire for warmth and yearn to burn the disconnection of the discontent souls

You speak truth, causing them to think and re-think their being

Challenging them to rise above their mellow humbug selves

You encourage greatness

To be the extra in ordinary

the power that is full

Because this is what you do. You can talk the talk, because you walk the walk

You embody what is true

If I could just step into your shoes

Beautiful Queen, your mind is so keen

Politics, education, relationships, love, and self-security you bring

You spit it all through your vernacular in speech

Watching you, hearing you, knowing you is such a treat

Sweet and calm, but meticulously battling word for word to overcome past battles of near defeat

If I could just step into your shoes

Be you for one day

Have so much to say

And be surrounded by people who want to listen

You walk with intention and true conviction

This is who I admire, and I listen

You have taught me so much though you are distant

Distant taking on the world, radiating, sharing your light, continue your fight

I love you and though I can't walk in your shoes

I will follow your lead and be the best me walking purposefully on my journey

Chapter 10
Man, That Is Not Mine

I've dreamed, pleaded, searched for you

Thug by nature which means your heart is true

Businessman but not white collared or blue

Oh, what I would sacrifice to love and receive love from you

You are a protector and a provider

Also, a real outsider

brilliant in mind

with a heart so kind

generous and loving

I didn't see you coming

easy on the eyes

and you're not like the other guys

Our encounter has been supernatural

Metaphysical

your words speak to my heart, my soul, the essence of my story

A man who is so real deserves the glory

But when it's all said and done,

You are taken

and dedicated you are to your manly duties

so, man who is not mine,

I love you dearly

But I must let the thought go

Maybe in another lifetime,

I can't help but hope

For a chance to allow our love to grow

Chapter 11
You

Stubborn, humorous, foolish you
conscience, caring, charming you
vivacious, flirtatious, demanding you
loveable, thoughtful, courageous you
childish, romantic, dramatic you
wanting, kissing, missing you

Chapter 12
Love Birth

Love tower of beauty

Foundation so solid

Creation gives birth to ideas

Once dreamed about

Partnership so true

My other half came out of the blue

But together we stand

Woman and Man

Ready to make our mark in the sand

He is my soul's friend

Thank you for taking my hand

Protecting, guiding, and nurturing

Like a real man

Chapter 13
From a Hopeful Romantic

Where are the men that love unconditionally?

kiss with passion,

speak with truth

stands by their word

And who are willing to protect and serve

Where are the men that appreciate a good woman?

builds her up, and pushes her towards success and excellence

Gentle and kind, considerate and true

Where are the men that cherish the good ones?

Who understands her value, and knows that his life is worthless
without her by his side

Where are the men who don't need to hide because he got something
on the side?

Where are the men that pay attention to her needs?

feeds her knowledge and knows how to read

Read in between the fine lines, so that he knows just what to do

when she gets in one of those crazy moods

Where are the men who always keep it real and true?

And who don't play her for a fool

Where are the men who don't play games with her heart?

Who knows how to give and receive without playing the part?

Where are the men who finish what they start?

Where are the men?

Because I'm ready to open my heart.....

Chapter 14
To Love a Woman

Love, Trust, authenticity

You are feeling the inner me

Not the glow of the outer beauty beholds

But allowing the truth of my identity to

Unfold

Hold me, caress me, love me

But most importantly

Delve deep into my soul

I am much more than a magical hole

I have magical powers that can help us

Both reach our goals

But first you must invest your time so that

We can mold

The foundation for the best love story

Ever told……

Love: I am thankful for the people in my life. They have taught me so many lessons on this journey. There are some people that I love and just genuinely admire because I can tell that they are operating out of love; whether it's love for life, love for their craft, love for people, or love for making a difference in the world. Thank you to all the people who choose to exist within a space of love.

Admiration: On my journey, I have always looked to find women mentors, and for some reason, it was tough because they were either dealing with their own insecurities or they felt a sense of intimidation from me. I would try so hard to connect with them, but nothing worked. There was this one girl who was close to my age and I just thought she was so amazing. She seemed like she had her stuff together. She was beautiful, articulate, ambitious, a natural leader and overall, she seemed like a good person. I asked her to be my mentor because I really admired her and her poetry. I admired the fact that she could confidently express her poetry to any crowd, while I kept all my work a secret. I think she was a little taken back by the fact that I wanted her to be my mentor and we were basically the same age. She said she would try, but we never kept in contact after that. Even so, I didn't take it personally, and to this day, I still admire her. At the time she exhibited the confidence that I wish I had. One thing I wish I would have done was just told her how much I admired her strength and passion.

As I got older, I started to realize the importance of letting people know how you feel. Speak life into people because even though she seemed on top of the world; you never know what a person is going through and how your kind words can make them feel. I'm sure she would have been more receptive to hearing my kind words rather than me randomly asking her to mentor me, even though we barely knew each other. However, I do encourage all women to identify positive mentors who can support you throughout your journey. For me, a couple of women were placed in my life and though I didn't directly ask them, I watched them and had deep conversations with them to try to learn how to develop some of their positive characteristics. Interestingly enough, I now have young girls who look at me with that same admiration and I don't wait for them to ask me to mentor them; I automatically take on that role because I know this is what the little girl inside, desires. Each one, reach one, and teach one to make this place a better world.

Chapter 15
Memory

You are what I hold on to keep me secure

You are what my existence depends

You hold my story in the palm of your hands

You know the happiest times with family and friends

You hold against me the bad times of frustration

You hold the power of future generations

You take with me the pain of life

You give back to me meaningful and purposeful insight

You are my beginning

My middle

My end

-You are my memory

Chapter 16
Slow Down

Slow down

Slow down to listen. Slow down to love

Slow down to appreciate a touch, a kiss, a hug

Slow down to be…. Slow down to learn

Slow down to enjoy me, you, him and her

Slow down to ponder. Slow down to wonder

Slow down to dream, wish, and imagine

Slow down to awaken the genie-like Aladdin

Slow down

Always moving, on the go, never slow

slow down or life will flash by because you never took the time to-

slow down

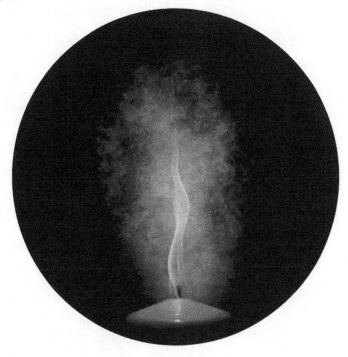

Chapter 17
Keep me Going

Motivate me to greatness...
Help me see me beyond my stress
Living life so full and freeeeeee
Baby-this-is where I want to be!

This world often drowns me
Consumes me into its sea of calamities
Save me from the darkness, madness, and emptiness
Take me, elevate me, keep me going strong
So hard so, push me far along
Show me, show me this is where I belong
Keep me, keep me, keep me going strong

Barriers don't exist
When you encourage me to the tenth!
So many people look to shred me into a box that I don't fit!
But with you by my side, their negativity I can resist
help me follow my heart and stay true to my own consensus.

Take me, elevate me, keep me going strong
So hard so hard so, push me far along
Show me, show me this is where I belong
Keep me, keep me, keep me going strong

Chapter 18
Wishing on a Star

I am wishing on the star

for beauty to unfold

nature vs nurture

the real behold

I wish on a star

for abundance, love and peace

inner vs outer

strength and release

I am wishing on a star

for guidance and the ability to be

old vs new

understanding the truth

I am wishing on a star

for all things that joy brings

passion vs desire

Allowing the burn of the fire

I am wishing on as star

For all those near and far

Chapter 19
Spiritual Awakening

Love full blown

peace of mind

throughout time

looking towards the future

life learned lessons

stand by truth, remember

Remember all that you are

And know all that you possess

You birth the life of creation

So live life without hesitation

And let the beauty unfold and

The power will result in manifestation

Affirmations: Some of my poems are written as affirmations, prayers, or motivational pieces. This is to affirm me of my power, who I am, and my birthright to accomplish my dreams. I use markers to write my affirmations down on my mirror and repeat them out loud to train my mind to focus on positivity. Think about some of the things you do to help you focus on the positive and what you desire out of life?

Chapter 20
Me

Intuitively silent about my approach
Sadness reigns within
But smiles appear when the real is presented
The inner light of my soul repented
the sorrowful nights no longer apply
Everything in me is amazingly gifted
Though fear arises from how I am depicted
Judge me, try to crush me, say what you will
I fight every day to overcome this fear
Lessons taught that the over-security of self
leads to the insecurity of me
But don't let my flaws fool you
For I have a gift for all to see

Chapter 21
Fear of the Unknown

Stepping into darkness

Not sure when I will find the light

But knowing that I must fight

Fight for my right to discover purpose

For being here on earth

Pushing forward into unknown waters

Getting wet, feeling as if I am drowning

Looking around hoping to be found

But there is no one there who can save me...

But me

I have the capabilities

Abilities to foresee

The plan was written before birth you see

Life of strife

Life of shine

I'm here to take back what's rightfully mine

So clear the way

Because my light is here to stay

Chapter 22
Internal Beauty

The beauty of me is the will to reach within to discover all that I am and that I can be

Beautiful heart, full of love, giving, receiving 'love unbound'

Never needing the spotlight, others can be forefront, but amazingly I take the lead

By discretely delegating and manipulating the formation of things

Can't deny the talented force that lives inside

Drive me to my full destiny

Allow me to give and receive the best of me

Chapter 23
Radiated by Divine Authority

I am a divine power

I am beauty within and outward

I am a manifestation of light, truth and love

I am centered to radiate light, truth and love

I am surrounded by positivity, creativity, love and abundance

I am surrounded and protected by love from family, friends and kindred spirits

I am imperfection evolving with each connection

Seeking my higher self

I attract beauty and greatness into my life

I am the personification of power, self-understanding, health, wellness, and wealth both spiritual and physical

I am surrounded by beauty in nature, my home is peaceful and serene, I always aim to be and look my best

Though I am greatness, I am humble and practice humility

I am T. Le Sure and much more

Chapter 24
Queen in Me

I'm a queen, but the way you come at me is so obscene

I mean what do you really mean.

addressing me as sexy, cutie, big booty, but I am not Judy

Don't you know who I am?

the beauty I possess within?

you're so shallow that you only see waist deep

but it's going to take more than a few words like hey boo what it do

for you to swim in this sea

First I need you to see, but not with your eyes

but with your soul

see all my lovable ways

the way I encourage, uplift, build guide and nurture

the way I love hard and give my time to help my sister and my brother

the way I stand tall in the face of adversity

the way I collect checks to feed the hungry

the gentleness with fierce undertones

my ability to take care of home

so you can poof be gone

because it's clear you don't see

all that I possess and all that I will be

What a blind visionary

I need a real King to see and understand......

the Queen in me

Chapter 25
Love?

Where does love to come from? How do I know that I am truly loving?

I want to open my heart to love life, to love people, to love animals, to love nature, to love all that life is

I want to enjoy peace and tranquility and have the understanding that in this state; love lives

I want to feel the unbound overflowing of love

God created beauty

He created light from the darkness

He created the birds, trees, animals and us out of love

I want to imitate Him and create from love

I know I can do it because He is me and I am Him and together we are love

Chapter 26
Writer's Block

Write…write…write. Right alright.

The struggle of a writer is he/she can write something so intently beautiful,

deep in meaning and eloquently put together…

and he/she knows they have the wonderful talent

but the writer gets stagnant in thought

impatient with the process of putting words together in manner that sparks the interest of another.

Then there's always that question of what am I going to write about? Where am I going with this writing?

How do I develop this idea?

So much goes into the writing process that it can often be daunting,

but once the writer gets into their zone,

magic happens

and the process becomes a beautiful moment in time,

released through the creative mind. --

Chapter 27
My Gift

I am a writer

so divine and true

I am a writer

look at the things I can do

I am a writer

I make you feel emotions of joy and pain

I am a writer

I am true to the game

I am a writer

This is where I will get my fame

I am a writer

Not everyone's gift is the same

Me: I have often struggled with feeling free to be me. I sometimes get so consumed with what others will think or how they will respond to me, but through constant self-discovery, I am learning to appreciate the beauty in me. We are all here for a reason, and it is our job to delve deep into our souls to uncover who we are. Embrace your struggles because it will make you stronger and they will take you to the depths of you. Embrace your flaws because they make you unique, and embrace you because you were created from love and the very fact that you are living is proof that your life has a significant purpose here on earth.

People often think having a degree, money, materialistic items, or a romantic partner defines you, but this is not true. If you lose all of these things at the end of the day, then what are you left with? You! So, it is essential to delve deep into you and appreciate your existence on earth. For years I've chased accomplishments to define me as a person. I graduated high school, went to college, worked multiple jobs while traveling in a hip-hop production and serving disadvantaged youth. I obtained my master's degree and went on to work in low socio-economic communities. I eventually landed a job as a teacher, then a specialized high school counselor making good money. Though all of this sounds great, it still didn't bring me the happiness I desired. It was not until I started asking myself who I am without all of my accomplishments or titles that I started to have an appreciation for me. Who am I? I am a strong woman who is compassionate, loving, ambitious, and I enjoy reflective writing. I work hard to be the best version of me and to help others be their most authentic self. I appreciate life, family, friends, and I am so grateful for my support system. I am not perfect, and I don't have to be. I can just be me, and that is good enough. This is a constant lesson that I continue to learn in life.

Insecurities: Living in such a judgmental world can be very tough, especially in a world of social media where it is hard to decipher the real from the fake. It's not just the outer world that judges and ridicules us; it is also our own family and friends. However, no one has ever judged me harder than I have judged myself. I've tried to hide behind a false perception of having it all together, but this was killing me inside. It wasn't until I learned the power of vulnerability that I started to release a lot of the facade and I began to connect genuinely with people. Surround yourself with people who will allow you to be you and who appreciate all that you are. Everyone has insecurities, but when you can embrace and accept all of you, then this is when you will begin practicing self-love, and the right people will gravitate towards you!

Authenticity Journal

My goal is to provide people with the opportunity to reflect on a deeper level. This section is for you to tap into your most authentic self and to process your thoughts and ideas about some of the topics discussed in this book. In the space below, write down whatever comes to mind when you are reading the poems. Feel free to be free! My only request is to be authentic in your responses. Enjoy!

What does it mean to be authentic? Do you feel you are someone who strives to be genuine and true to yourself? Please describe or give examples of the type of person you are and who you aim to be? In a world that is often full of so many people who are trying to be who they are not, why is authenticity important?

The first few poems in my book, expresses my internal struggles dealing with so many insecurities and uncertainties about myself. While people viewed me as having it all together, I viewed myself as a mess. My low self-esteem caused me to seek validation from outside sources, like men and social media. What internal issues do you struggle with or do you feel women in general are struggling with? Do you look for validation from the outside world and why?

Now, reflect on the things that you value about yourself. List as many great qualities as possible. Then, ask three people closest to you to identify at least ten positive things about you. Please take the time to do this as silly as it may seem. Sometimes, we don't know just how wonderful we are in the eyes of those who are closest to us.

Have you ever had an experience of heartbreak? Please write about a time when you felt trapped or unhappy in a relationship. It may even be in a current relationship. Describe your feelings and how this relationship has affected you. Let it all out! There is a second therapeutic part to this process, so please be authentic in your response.

Now that you have released the negative aspects of the relationship, write down any of the positives that stemmed from this relationship. Then, please take the time to create a new narrative. Re-write your story to re-program your mind, but write it in terms of what you would have liked to happen in this relationship? Write down how you want to feel in your current or future relationship? In order to get to the point of having a successful and fulfilling partnership, it is important that you are in-tune with yourself, you understand your needs, and that you are able to communicate this to your partner. It can be a transformative experience to write out and visualize the relationship you desire to have. Always remember, that a healthy and happy relationship begins with a healthy and authentically happy, you!

Please write about something that you would like to heal from. In my book, I talked about a few things that empowered me to heal through some of the painful experiences in my life. What steps are you taking to heal yourself or what are some possible steps that you can take to begin the healing process? It is ok if you don't know what steps to take, but please ask for help from a person you trust or feel free to email me. Don't be ashamed. At times, we all need a little bit of support.

In my conversations with women, we often talk bad about the hurt that men have caused us. For this reason, I think it is important to identify the positive attributes of the men who are or were in our lives. Take some time to reflect on three or more men who you have learned valuable lessons from, and identify what you admire or appreciate about them. It's so important that we don't get caught in a bitter mind-set towards men. When we begin to focus on the positive, we bring more positivity into our lives.

Please take the time to write out the names of at least three women who have had a positive influence on your life. Describe how they have impacted your life and the beautiful qualities they possess. By doing this, you will start to see and understand some of your own values and it will allow you to exude these qualities for others.

We are all in different stages in our lives. In my book, it begins to tell a story about a young woman who feels lost and confused about her place in life. It then tackles themes such as toxic relationships, to slowly beginning to appreciate life and the people in it, and finally learning important lessons about self-love. In addition, there are messages about understanding your strengths, gifts, and talents so that you can walk in your purpose. Please take some time to write about the current stage that you are in during this time of your life. In addition, write out the gifts and talents you possess and how you will utilize these gifts to walk in your purpose and operate in your power!

Thank you for taking the time to exist in authenticity!

Final Thoughts

"Life is a beautifully unwritten script."

Embrace the challenges, because they are making you stronger and wiser.

Cherish the good people in your life because they will help carry you through the dark times, and they will bring you endless joy through the good times.

Forgive the people who have hurt you because they have allowed you to understand what it means to be human. To forgive those who hurt you, is to set yourself free from the pain, disappointment, and anger they left behind.

Appreciate every moment in time.

Be authentically you because the world needs you!

#womensupportingwomen

CPSIA information can be obtained
at www.ICGtesting.com
Printed in the USA
FSHW011250041219
64753FS